Sr. Patricia

Carmelite Monastery

1381 University Ave.

N. Y 52 - N.y.

Pray for

F. D. M.

Figures for an
Apocalypse

Published by
NEW DIRECTIONS
Norfolk, Connecticut

FIGURES
FOR AN
APOCALYPSE

by

Thomas

Merton

Some of these poems first appeared in *The Commonweal, Spirit, Sewanee Review, The Western Review, Voices, The Tiger's Eye;* and the essay, *Poetry and the Contemplative Life,* was printed in *The Commonweal.*

NEW DIRECTIONS, 500 FIFTH AVENUE, NEW YORK CITY 18

Ex Parte Ordnis:

Nihil Obstat   FR. M. GABRIEL O'CONNELL, D. C. S. O.
                       FR. M. ANTHONY CHASSAGNE, O. C. S. O.

Imprimi Potest   FR. M. DOMINIQUE NOGUES, O. C. S. O.
                          Abbas Generalis

———

Nihil Obstat   JOHN M. A. FEARNS, S. T. D.
                          Censor Librorum

Imprimatur   ✠   FRANCIS CARDINAL SPELLMAN
                          Archbishop of New York

June 2, 1947

CONTENTS

Figures for an
Apocalypse

"And at midnight there was a cry made: Behold, the Bridegroom cometh, go ye forth to meet Him."

FIGURES FOR AN APOCALYPSE

I

Come down, come down Beloved
And make the brazen waters burn beneath Thy feet.

The mountains shine like wax,
And the cliffs, for fear of Thy look,
Gleam like sweet wax.
Thine eyes are furnaces;
The fireproof rocks unbar their adamantine banks
And weep like wax,
Spilling their diamonds and their emeralds.

Come down, come down Beloved
From the towers of Thy abode.

The waters shine like tin
In the alarming light.
The seas all ring their bells of steel
Beneath Thy terrible feet,
And the mountains quiver like rubber
To the drums of Thy tread.

For, from the beginning of the world,
How few of us have have heard the silver of Thy creed
Or paid our hearts for hours of emptiness
With gold of Thy belief?

The eyes that will not coin Thy Incarnation
Figured in every field and flowering tree—

How shall they pay for the drink of those last lights
Poured out on them that expect Thee?

Splitting the seven countries
With the prism of Thy smile,
Confound all augury:
Sever the center of our continents
And through that unpredictable gate lead in
The world's last night,
Clad in the wrath of Armageddon
And in Thy fires arrayed.

Light, then, Thy way to us between the kindled cities
And wake us with Thy trumpet's nine-mile cry,
Forging our minds with the too clear,
Too sudden "BRIDEGROOM!" bright as iron.

And Thou, in the armor of Thy creed's most solemn
        articles,
Rising tremendous in the black gates of death's
        empty Senegal,
Lead out Thy Bride still breathless with dazzle of
        release,
Still fluttering with the ribbons of the cities'
        mile-long flames
And we, (oh glad!)
Find we our kept, our tended lamps,
Secret amid the dinning herds of the alarum;
While Sidon and the walls of Tyre
Wet as the wax backs of the hog-hundreds, once,
        among the Gadarenes,
Fall down and drown in foaming seas.

Come to your windows, rich women,
Rise up in your rooms
And come to your windows, queens!

> "We have walked up and down the splendid
>   marble
>   Strict as compasses,
>   And viewed our shadows along the dining
>   rooms,
> Upon the clean, expensive stone."

Come to your doors, rich women.
Weep in the doors of your treasuries,
You thin, unprofitable queens:
Weep for the bangles on your jeweled bones.

> "We have stood in the late light
> Of the most lonely afternoons,
> And counted all the hours that accused us
> Cutting to the division of the marrow and the
>   spine."

How long has silence flourished
In the houses of their joy?
See, now, the broken window panes
Sing to them in their years without harvest
Keener than a violin!

"Why do you still wear
The dead gauds of your Mardi-Gras,

Crabbing in the unquiet noises of the dawn,
Grey, artificial Shebas, spurious queens?"

"We had not planned to have so great a Lent
Bind us and bite us with its heavy chain!"

Shall the Spirit be poured out upon this land?
Shall ever life swell up again in the drained veins,
As wild as wine?

Come to your windows, rich women;
Die in the doors of your need, you starving queens:
"For the vintage is at an end,
The gathering shall come no more."

III

*(Advice to my Friends Robert Lax and Edward Rice,
to get away while they still can.)*

Down at the Hotel Sherlock Holmes,
The walls being full of ears,
We sit with eyes as bright as milk
Writing our snow-white messages
To the lords of the bloody prison:
How shall we bargain a reprieve,
Win pity for the poor pilgrims,
Or forge a paper to Paradise
From the gates of the smouldering jail?
Shall they condemn all joy to die
In the jaws of this cat-and-dog harbor?

Down at the Fauntleroy Bar
With brimstone in our sorry drink,
We sit with eyes as sharp as stones
Writing our names in code—
Fearing to look where the windows ache
With the sight of the Babylon beast.
The skylights of our intellect
Have gone as grey as frost,
While the dawn makes ready, with coated tongue,
To mutter the last alarm:
We'd ask the man for a time-table
But the time-tables are all gone:
And so we sit with eyes like towers
In the hour of the final train.

Down at the Hotel Wonderland
With eyes as mad as rocks,
We swear at the wine as blue as fire
In the glass of our phony grail.
Oh, the despot touts are ripping their collars,
Cursing the atmosphere.
It is too late to fly away
From the city full of sulphur,
From the wide walks where antichrist
Slips us his cruel snare.
The dawn bides like a basilisk
In the doors of the Frankenstein building,
And the cops come down the street in fours
With clubs as loud as bells.

Time, time to go to the terminal
And make the escaping train

17

With eyes as bright as palaces
And thoughts like nightingales.
It is the hour to fly without passports
From Juda to the mountains,
And hide while cities turn to butter
For fear of the secret bomb.
We'll arm for our own invisible battle
In the wells of the pathless wood
Wounding our limbs with prayers and Lent,
Shooting the traitor memory
And throwing away our guns—
And learning to fight like Gedeon's men,
Hiding our lights in jugs.

IV

(*Cf. Apoc.* XIV, 14.)

Look in the night, look, look in the night:
Heaven stands open like a little temple,
With a man in the door
Having a sickle in his hand.

The steel is cleaner than ice,
The blade is sharper than thought:
The curve is like an intellect, neat!
He lifts up the sickle, and the stars cry out in alarm.
Look in the night, look, look in the night:
The man in the silver garment
Steps down from heaven's temple door.
The seas of the dark world
Boil to the brim with fear.
He raises the sickle. The blade flashes like a cry.

He thrusts in the sickle
And it begins to sing like wind
In the most quiet harvest of the midnight world.

Fly, fly to the mountains!
The temple door is full of angels.
Fly, fly to the hills!
The men on the red horses wait with guns
Along the blue world's burning brim!

The sickle rings like breezes
In harvesting this sleepy world,
Flashing and falling light as music.
There are a thousand angels standing in the gateway
    of the heaven-temple,
Viewing this voiceless harvesting.

Then, suddenly, comes the real dread, the real sound.
From out the empty universe,
Beyond the infinite air, the high star-spirals,
Out of the core of some far furious trumpet
The first wild note begins to spring,
And fires its anger, in an instant, through the ranks
Of the attending angels,
And bites my soul with lightnings live as steel!

V

Landscape, Prophet and Wild-dog

    The trees stand like figures in a theatre.
Then suddenly there comes a prophet, running for
    his life,

And the wild-dog behind him.
And now the wild-dog has him by the ankle
And the man goes down.

"Oh prophet, when it was afternoon you told us:
'Tonight is the millenium,
The withering-away of the state.
The skies, in smiles, shall fold upon the world,
Melting all injustice in the rigors of their
  breezy love.'
And all night long we waited at the desert's edge,
Hearing this wild-dog, only, on the far mountain,
Watching the white moon giggle in the stream!"

The two trees stand like Masters of Arts
And observe the wild-dog
Nailing his knives into the prophet's shoulder.

"Oh prophet, when it was night you came and
  told us:
'Tomorrow is the millenium,
The golden age!
The human race will wake up
And find dollars growing out of the palms of
  their hands,
And the whole world will die of brotherly love
Because the factories jig like drums
And furnaces feed themselves,
And all men lie in idleness upon the quilted
  pastures,
Tuning their friendly radios and dreaming in
  the sun!"

"But when the grey day dawned
What flame flared in the jaws of the avenging
    mills!
We heard the clash of hell within the gates of
    the embattled Factory
And thousands died in the teeth of those
    sarcastic fires!"

"And now the rivers are poisoned,
The skies rain blood
And all the springs are brackish with the taste
Of these your prophecies.
Oh prophet, tell us plainly, at last:
When is the day of our success?"

But there is no answer in the dead jaws.
And the air is full of wings.
The crows come down and sit like senators
On the arms of the two trees.

At the edge of the salt-lands
In the dry-blue clay
The wild-dog, with a red claw scuffs out a little
    hollow,
Burying the prophet's meatless shin.

VI

In the Ruins of New York

The moon is paler than an actress.
We have beheld her mourning in the brown ivy
Of the dendric bridges,—
In the brown, broken ivy
That loves but a span of air.

The moon is paler than an actress, and weeps for you,
    New York,
Seeking to see you through the tattered bridges,
Leaning down to catch the sham brass
Of your sophisticated voice,
Whose songs are heard no more!

Oh how quiet it is after the black night
When flames out of the clouds burned down your
    cariated teeth,
And when those lightnings,
Lancing the black boils of Harlem and the Bronx,
Spilled the remaining prisoners,
(The tens and twenties of the living)
Into the trees of Jersey,
To the green farms, to find their liberty.

How are they down, how have they fallen down
Those great strong towers of ice and steel,
And melted by what terror and what miracle?
What fires and lights tore down,
With the white anger of their sudden accusation,
Those towers of silver and of steel?

You whose streets grew up on trellisses
With roots in Bowling Green and tap-roots in the
    Upper Bay:
How are you stripped, now, to your skeleton:
What has become of your live and dead flesh:
Where is the shimmer of your bawdy leaves?
Oh, where your children in the evening of your
    final Sunday

Gunned after one another in the shadows of the
    Paramount,
The ashes of the levelled towers still curl with tufts
    of smoke
Veiling your obsequies in their incinerating haze
They write, in embers, this your epitaph:

    "This was a city
    That dressed herself in paper money.
    She lived four hundred years
    With nickles running in her veins.
    She loved the waters of the seven purple seas,
    And burned on her own green harbor
    Higher and whiter than ever any Tyre.
    She was as callous as a taxi;
    Her high-heeled eyes were sometimes blue as gin,
    And she nailed them, all the days of her life,
    Through the hearts of her six million poor.
    Now she has died in the terrors of a sudden
        contemplation
    ——Drowned in the waters of her own, her
        poisoned well."

Can we console you, stars,
For the so long survival of such wickedness?
Tomorrow and the day after
Grasses and flowers will grow
Upon the bosom of Manhattan.
And soon the branches of the hickory and sycamore
Will wave where all those dirty windows were—
Ivy and the wild-grape vine
Will tear those weak walls down,

Burying the brownstone fronts in freshness and
    fragrant flowers;
And the wild-rose and the crab-apple tree
Will bloom in all those silent mid-town dells.

There shall be doves' nests, and hives of bees
In the cliffs of the ancient apartments,
And birds shall sing in the sunny hawthorns
Where was once Park Avenue.
And where Grand Central was, shall be a little hill
Clustered with sweet, dark pine.

Will there be some farmer, think you,
Clearing a place in the woods,
Planting an acre of bannering corn
On the heights above Harlem forest?
Will hunters come explore
The virgin glades of Broadway for the lynx and deer?
Or will some hermit, hiding in the birches, build
    himself a cell
With the stones of the city hall,
When all the caved-in subways turn to streams
And creeks of fish,
Flowing in sun and silence to the reedy Battery?

But now the moon is paler than a statue.
She reaches out and hangs her lamp
In the iron trees of this destroyed Hesperides.
And by that light, under the caves that once were
    banks and theaters,
The hairy ones come out to play—
And we believe we hear the singing of the manticores

Echo along the rocks of Wall and Pine

And we are full of fear, and muter than the
    upside-down stars
That limp in the lame waters,
Muter than the mother moon who, white as death,
Flies and escapes across the wastes of Jersey.

VII

Landscape: Beast

Yonder, by the eastward sea
Where smoke melts in a saucer of extinguished cities,
The last men stand, in delegations,
Waiting to see the seven-headed business
Promised us, from those unpublished deeps:
Waiting to see those horns and diadems
And hear the seven voices of the final blasphemy.

And westward, where the other waters are as slick as
    silk
And slide, in the grey evening, with uncertain lights,
(Screened by the smoke of the extinguished studios)
The last men wait to see the seven-headed thing.
They stand around the radios
Wearing their regalia on their thin excited breasts,
Waving the signals of their masonry.
What will happen, when they see those heads,
    those horns
Dishevel the flickering sea?

How will they bare their foreheads, and put forth
    their hands
And wince with the last indelible brand,
And wear the dolour of that animal's number,
And evermore be burned with her disgusting name?

Inland, in the lazy distance, where a dozen planes
    still play
As loud as horseflies, round the ruins of an average
    town,
A blue-green medium dragon, swimming in the river,
Emerges from the muddy waters, comes to romp
    awhile upon the land.
She rises on the pathless shore,
And goes to roll in the ashes of the ravaged country.
But no man turns to see and be surprised
Where those grey flanks flash palely in the sun.
Who shall gather to see an ordinary dragon, in this
    day of anger,
Or wonder at those scales as usual as sin?

Meanwhile, upon the broken mountains of the south
No one observes the angels passing to and fro:
And no one sees the fire that shoots beneath the hoofs
Of all the white, impatient horses.

And no one hears or fears the music of those
    blazing swords.

(Northward, northward, what lies there to see?
Who shall recount the terror of those ruined streets?

And who shall dare to look where all the birds with
    golden beaks
Stab at the blue eyes of the murdered saints?)

VIII

The Heavenly City

City, when we see you coming down,
Coming down from God
To be the new world's crown:
How shall they sing, the fresh, unsalted seas
Hearing your harmonies!

For there is no more death,
No need to cure those waters, now, with any brine;
Their shores give them no dead,
Rivers no blood, no rot to stain them.

Because the cruel algebra of war
Is now no more.
And the steel circle of time, inexorable,
Bites like a padlock shut, forever,
In the smoke of the last bomb:
And in that trap the murderers and sorcerers and
    crooked leaders
Go rolling home to hell.
And history is done.

Shine with your lamb-light, shine upon the world:
You are the new creation's sun.
And standing on their twelve foundations,

Lo, the twelve gates that are One Christ are wide
     as canticles:
And Oh! Begin to hear the thunder of the songs
     within the crystal Towers,
While all the saints rise from their earth with feet
     like light
And fly to tread the quick-gold of those streets,

Oh City, when we see you sailing down,
Sailing down from God,
Dressed in the glory of the Trinity, and angel-crowned
In nine white diadems of liturgy.

LANDSCAPE: WHEATFIELDS

Frown there like Cressy or like Agincourt,
You fierce and bearded shocks and sheaves
And shake your grain-spears,
And know no tremor in your vigilant
Your stern array, my summer chevaliers!

Although the wagons,
(Hear how the battle of those wheels,
Worrying the loose wood with their momentary
    thunder
Leaves us to guess some trestle, there, behind the
    sycamores,)
Although the empty wagons come,

Rise up, like kings out of the pages of a chronicle
And cry your courage in your golden beards;
For now the summer-time is half-way done,
Gliding to a dramatic crisis
Sure as the deep waters to the sedentary mill.

Arise like kings and prophets from the pages of
    an ancient Bible,
And blind us with the burnish of your message
    in our June:
Then raise your hands and bless us
And depart, like old Melchisedech, and find your
    proper Salem.

The slow hours crowd upon us.

Our days slide evenly toward the term of all
          our liturgy,
And all our weeks are after Pentecost.

Summer divides his garrisons,
Surrenders up his strongest forts,
Strikes all his russet banners one by one.
And while these ancient men of war
Casting us in the teeth with the reproof of their
          surrender
(By which their fruitfulness is all fulfilled,)
Throw down their arms,

Face we the day when we go up to stake our graces
Against unconquerable God:
Try, with our trivial increase, in that time of harvest
To stem the army of His attributes!

Oh pray us full of marrow, Queen of Heaven,
For those mills, His truth, our glory!
Crown us with alleluias on that day of fight!

(Light falls as fair as lyres, beamy between the
          branches,
Plays like an angel on the mill-dam, where the lazy
          stream
Suddenly turns to clouds of song and rain,)
Oh pray us, Lady, full of faith and graces,
Arm us wih fruits against that contest and
          comparison,
Arm us with ripeness for the wagons of our Christ!

TWO STATES OF PRAYER

In wild October when the low hills lie
With open eye
And own the land like lions,

Our prayer is like the thousands in the far,
    forgotten stadiums,
Building its exultation like a tower of fire,
Until the marvelous woods spring to their feet
And raid the skies with their red-headed shout:

This is the way our hearts take flame
And burn us down, on pyres of prayer, with too
    much glory.

But when the trees have all torn up their programs,
Scattering the pathos of immense migrations to the
    open-handed winds,
Clouding and saddening the dusky valley,
Sorrow begins to bully the bare bars
Of those forsaken cages
As thought lies slaughtered in the broken doors.

But by the light of our December mornings,
Though words stand frozen in the voice's well
And all the country pumps are dumb,
Look where the landscape, like a white Cistercian,
Puts on the ample winter like a cowl

31

And so conceals, beneath the drifts as deep as
        quietude,
The ragged fences and the ravaged field.

The hills lie still, the woods their Sabbath keep.
The farms, half buried in their winter coats
Are warm as sheep.
When was there ever greater than this penitential
        peace
Outshining all the songs of June with radiant silences?

November analyzed our bankruptcies, but now
His observations lie knee-deep beneath our
        Christmas mercies,
While folded in the buried seed
The virtual summer lives and sleeps;
And every acre keeps its treasure like a kingly secret.

A LETTER TO AMERICA

America, when you were born, and when the plains
Spelled out their miles of praises in the sun
What glory and what history
The rivers seemed to prepare.

We hear them, now, in the Kentucky summer,
While all the locusts drown our forests in their iron
      prayer:
And we dream of you, beloved, sleeping in your
      leafy bosom.

How long are we to wake
With eyes that turn to wells of blood
Seeing the hell that gets you from us
With his treacherous embrace!

The bands that raced our flesh
With smiles as raw as scars,
Can kill you, Kansas, with their high-powered thirst.
Have you not heard the vast Missouri sing
To drown them with those billion gallon silences?

But when the day is quieter
Than your primeval cradle
All our green woods fill, once again, with wishful lies:
Maybe the cities, (sing the birds, our travellers)
Maybe the cities have begun to heal,
And stanched their smoky hemorrhage:
Maybe they have begun to mend their cauteries,
Parsing the muteness of so many dead.

Down where the movies grit
Their white electric teeth,
Maybe the glorious children have rebelled
And rinsed their mental slums
In the clean drench of an incalculable grief.

Maybe their penitence has torn the phony sunset
To view their devil dressed in laudanum,
And scotched his crazy spectre,
And learned the liberty of the unfathomable stars,
Within the doors of their confessionals,
Their new, more lasting Lexingtons!

But oh! the flowering cancers of that love
That eats your earth with roots of steel!
No few fast hours can drain your flesh
Of all those seas of candied poison,

Until our long Gregorian cry
Bows down the stars' Samaritan
To rue the pity of so cruel a murder.

THREE POSTCARDS FROM THE
MONASTERY

I

The pilgrim passes swiftly.
All the strange towns,
Wrapped in their double cloaks
(Of rain and of non-entity)
Veil their elusive faces.

The pale world, white as plaster,
(Its doors are dumb, its windows far too blind for
     lamentation)
Dies like problematical news.

We have receded from the things
You printed on those unidentified facades.
We barely dream about the frontispiece
Of your collapsing palaces.
We can refuse your tin.

The smoky choirs
Of those far five-o'clock trombones
Have blown away. Our eyes
Are clean as the September night.
Our minds, (our silences) are light years deep.

Who shall amaze us with the noise of your
     discovery, America?
Who shall make known to us your new, true name,
Instead of knocking at our gates,

Bidding us look again upon that blank and pictured
    concentration?

Because the ticker-tapes are dead,
The radios are all shot:
But we have gone up to buy you Andromeda.

II

It is because the sun
Shines on the shallows like a cannonade
That we have come inland.

It is because the cloudy sea
Hailing the cliffs as loud as promises,
Saluting all the continent with foaming orchestras,

Raided the shore with tons of silver
That we have fled to the penniless hills,
Hidden in the poor, laborious fields.

We stood one moment by the bridgehead of those
    fatal fortunes:
Days that offered to fill our hands with gold,
Surfs that crowded the grey rocks with ballyhoo.

Shall I speak plain against the sun?
Or sing together with the comic-operas of the sea?
We have refused the reward,
We have abandoned the man-hunt.
But when the contest is over
We shall inherit the world.

III

Once were begotten
In the wombs of the deep mountains:
Born over and over in the play of penitential
  tunnels.
Such was our birth and resurrection from the
  freezing east
The night we cleared you, Pittsburgh, in a maze
  of lights.

Our lives were suddenly weaned in strange Ohio,
(Whose towns made little love to us, in their green
  requiems)
Weaned from the land and atmosphere of men.

Have you ever heard this music
Sung over and over by night,
How we will live *in loco pascuae?*
Or the assuring voices of those inward violins
Play: "Going to Gethsemani?"

(We were begotten in the tunnels of December rain,
Born from the wombs of news and tribulation,
By night, by wakeful rosary:
Such was my birth, my resurrection from the freezing
  east,
The night we cleared you, Cincinnati, in a maze
  of lights.)

ON THE ANNIVERSARY OF MY BAPTISM

Certain waters are as blue as metal
Or as salt as sorrow.
Others wince like brass in the hammering sun,
Or stammer all over with tremors of shadow
That die as fast as the light winds
Whose flights surprise the promontories
And the marble bay.

Some are crowded everywhere, off-shore, with
        purple coral
Between the fleets of light that founder in the sand.
Others are full of yawls, or loud with launches,
Or sadder than the bitter smoke
Of tug and trawler, tramp and collier,

Or as grey as battle.

Oh! Since I was a baby in the Pyrenees,
When old St. Martin marked me for the cloister
        from high Canigou,

How many deeps, how many wicked seas
Went to befriend me with a flash of white-caps
Louder than laughter in the wind and sun,
Or sluggered all our brown bows gunwale-under
In their rowdy thunder—
Only to return me to the land.

Do you suppose that if the green Atlantic

Had ever cracked our brittle shell
And rifled all the cabins for their fruit of drunken
    passengers,
Do you suppose my sins,
Once we were sorted and disposed forever
Along the shelves of that profound, unvisited museum,
Would there have been immune,
Or learned to keep their coats of unreality
From the deep sea's most patient candying?

The day You made the waters,
And dragged them down from the dividing islands
And made them spring with fish,
You planned to bless the brine out of the seas
That were to be my death.

And this is the ninth November since my world's
    end and my Genesis,
When, with the sting of salt in my dry mouth,
Cross-crowned with water by the priest,
Stunned at the execution of my old companion, death,
And with the murder of my savage history,
You drowned me in the shallow font.

My eyes, swimming in unexpected infancy,
Were far too frail for such a favor:
They still close-kept the stone shell of their empty
    sepulchre:
But, though they saw none, guessed the new-come
    Trinity
That charged my sinews with His secret life.

SONG: CONTEMPLATION

O land alive with miracles!
O clad in streams,
Countering the silver summer's pleasant arrows
And beating them with the kind armor
Of your enkindled water-vesture,

Lift your blue trees into the early sun!

O country wild with talent
Is there an hour in you that does not rouse our mind
    with songs?
The boughs that bend in the weak wind
Open us momentary windows, here and there,
Into those deep and purple galleries,
Disclosing us the birds your genius;

And yet the earth is loud
With more than this their timid vaudeville.

O brilliant wood!
Yours is the voice of a new world;
And all the hills burn with such blinding art

That Christ and angels walk among us, everywhere.
These are their ways, their fiery footsteps,
That flash and vanish, smile and pass;
——By those bright passengers our groves are all
    inspired.
Lo, we have seen you, we have seized you, wonder,

Caught you, half held you in the larch and lighted
    birch:
But in that capture you have sailed us half-mile-high
    into the air
To taste the silences of the inimitable hawk:

Nor do we swing upon the wind
To scan the flattened barns as brown as blood
Growing into the surface of the wounded earth,
Or learn the white roads, livid as a whipcut scar.
For suddenly we have forgotten your geography,
Old nature, and your map of prey,
And know no more the low world scourged with
    travelling.

The genuine steps, the obvious degrees
The measured cart-ways and the fields we trod all day
And the tunes of the clattering shops,
Even the songs that crowned the highest hill
Find us no longer beggars for their petty coin.
We've left the stations of the mendicants
And the ways of the workaday saints.

But in the dazzled, high and unelectric air
Seized in the talons of the terrible Dove,
The huge, unwounding Spirit,
We suddenly escape the drag of earth
Fly from the dizzy paw of gravity
And swimming in the wind that lies beyond the track
Of thought and genius and of desire,

Trample the white, appalling stratosphere.

A MYSTERIOUS SONG IN THE SPRING OF THE YEAR

In April, when our land last died
And secrecy rebelled against the sun,
And hidden heaven mocked the visible systems
With white untouchable flowers,

Old Duty, sitting at his beggarpost,
Counted the changes of the sun-and-water season:
All spattered, there, behind the willow's greening
    shower.
Now it was he who tried to woo us to the purchase
Of accurate annals of our state,
Waking, upon our passage, with a musical cry.
But we refused his all too faithful history.

What exorcist
Had stilled you, five commercial senses,
And locked away your lion-light
And saved our capture from those bleeding paws?
Or into what division had we slipped,
Figured in what oblique escape,
Sidelong into eternity, between the angular hour?

The bells were ever at their belfry-place,
Quarter by quarter rang us to our busy death,
Reckoning-up our obligations
In the high tower's teller-cages:

But we with work too suddenly done
And locked in a trice to the unexpected Cross

Had died and gone our way, ten, twenty years
    ahead of the appointed time.

Oh, life, put down your organ-grinder's cup,
Tax us no more, greyfellow, for our ears are
    shuttered:
Our eyes are dark, but we are not asleep:
Our hands are folded where we work, in state,
    in requie.

Oh happy death, where life and fright,
Where love and loss are drawn apart
And stand, forever, separate,
While one by one the fragments of a century
Disintegrate and fall in silence all about us:
And these are news of peace, but not dismay,

For heaven is builded deeper and stronger everywhere
From the collapse of our neglected history.

CANTICLE FOR THE BLESSED VIRGIN

Die, Boreas,
And drown your ruins in the gaudy sea,
December, clash your cymbals once again
And put them away.
The crops come thronging from the ground.
The land is green with strength.
The harvests sing like confidence
In the ascetic earth.
Let there be no more patience
With your iron music, death:
Stand, continents, and wear the spring your crown!

The ox-eyed land,
The muted lakes,
The cloudy groves that praise you, Lady, with their
        blooms,
Fuse and destroy their lights
And burn them into gold for you, great Virgin,
Coining your honor in the glorious sun.

The skies speed up to meet you, and the seas
Swim you the silver of their crests.
If you delay to come, we'll see the meteors, by night,
Skimming before your way,
Lighting the time of death's dismay
In lights as lithe as animals.
And God will blaze your pathway with the
        incandescent stars.

But oh! Queen of all grace and counsel,
Cause of our joy, Oh Clement Virgin, come:
Show us those eyes as chaste as lightning,
Kinder than June and true as Scripture.
Heal with your looks the poisons of the universe,
And claim your Son's regenerate world!

Because your Christ disposed Orion and
    Andromeda
And ordered the clean spheres,
And interplayed the chiming suns to be your toy,
Charm you with antiphon and psalmody
And canticle, and countersong;

Because your Christ
Fired the fair stars with argent for your raiment,
And charged the sinner's tears
With clean repentent lights——
(As on the day you found me in the dens of libraries
And crushed the jeweled head of heresy)——
He gave you every one of the redeemed to be your
    dowry
And angels for your crown.

Come from the compass quarter where the thunder
    sleeps
And let the pity of those eyes
Rout all the armies of our million dangers
Here where we lie in siege:
For you unlock the treasures of the bleeding Wood.
You hold the Mass-keys, and the locks of Calvary,
And All-grace springs in the founts of your demand.

45

II

Lady, whose smiles are full of counsel and theology,
Never have you withheld those seas of light
Whose surf confounds the keenest eye.
Grace me to be the soldier of your Scotus,
Arming my actions with the news
Of your Immaculate command.

You, who have saved me from the ones about to
    break me
On the iron wheels of sin,
And bought me from the torturer
With all the florins of the Parasceve:
If Christ will burn me clean
Of my red-handed perjuries,
Win me His Blood again, and blazon me His priest.

But if my hands that one time wore the stench of
    death
Are too unworthy of the Liturgy
That speaks our deathless Pasch in veils of Bread,
Make me, until my death, His priest in secret
Offering Mass in all-day's sacrifice.

Teach me to take all grace
And spring it into blades of act,
Grow spears and sheaves of charity,
While each new instant, (new eternity)
Flowering with clean and individual circumstance,
Speaks me the whisper of His consecrating Spirit.
Then will obedience bring forth new Incarnations
Shining to God with the features of His Christ.

46

Envoi:

Tower, stars, and oh! you sun in Aries,
Shatter a way for her through the embattled weather,
Until the hills
Tidy their fields, and fill them full of flowers
For those Annunciations:

And hell shall melt his onsets
Faster than January's brawling clouds
Doomed by the music of her chariot.

DUNS SCOTUS

Striking like lightning to the quick of the real world
Scotus has mined all ranges to their deepest veins:
But where, oh, on what blazing mountain of theology
And in what Sinai's furnace
Did God refine that gold?

Who ruled those arguments in their triumphant order
And armed them with their strict celestial light?
See the lance-lightning, blade-glitter, banner-progress
As love advances, company by company
In sunlit teams his clean embattled reasons,

Until the firmament, with high heavenly marvel
Views in our crystal souls her blue embodiment,
Unfurls a thousand flags above our heads——
It is the music of Our Lady's army!

For Scotus is her theologian,
Nor has there ever been a braver chivalry than his
          precision.
His thoughts are skies of cloudless peace
Bright as the vesture of her grand aurora
Filled with the rising Christ.

But we, a weak, suspicious generation,
Loving emotion, hating prayer,
We are not worthy of his wisdom.
Creeping like beasts between the mountain's feet
We look for laws in the Arabian dust.
We have no notion of his freedom

Whose acts despise the chains of choice and passion.
We have no love for his beatitude
Whose act renounces motion:
Whose love flies home forever
As silver as felicity,
Working and quiet in the dancelight of an
    everlasting arrow.

Lady, the image of whose heaven
Sings in the might of Scotus' reasoning:
There is no line of his that has not blazed your glory
    in the schools,
Though in the dark words, without romance,
Calling us to swear you our liege.

Language was far too puny for his great theology:
But, oh! His thought strode through those words
Bright as the conquering Christ
Between the clouds His enemies:
And in the clearing storm, and Sinai's dying thunder
Scotus comes out, and shakes his golden locks
And sings like the African sun.

TWO DESERT FATHERS

I

St. Jerome

The light that rises on Jehosaphat
Greyer than the rocks
On which the Baptist stood and preached,
Showed you the coming of the solemn Christ.
You heard His speech proceding like an army
Before Whose tread all understanding shall succumb
Knowing no way of withstanding the weight of
    His language
Or the keen, bright, two-way sword-measure
Of that Judgment.

The light that sank upon the valley of the final
    settlement
Showed you over and over the wreckage of the
    universe
Boiling like wine out of the faucets of that ruined
    stadium
Far bloodier than the vintage of those evenings
    in the trampled west.

Jerome! Jerome!
What is this voice comes down to us
Down the far tunnels from the heaven of your
    solitude?
You who have died hard by the caves of Bethlehem

Forgotten by the barren world, the hater of the
    Incarnation,
Oh, now, how suddenly risen again
You chide us with that language loud with fight:
Language of one who had to wrestle in the long
    night's wilderness
With the wild angel, Revelation.

Words were not made to dress such lightning
And thought cracks under the pressure of that thunder
When your most learned, mad
And immaculate indignation

Sunders with its meteors the darkness of our classic
    intellection,
Severs our midnight like a streak of flying pullmans
And challenges our black unhappiness
Loud as the lights of an express.

II

St. Paul the Hermit

When Egypt dies behind a hundred miles of heat
And the low Nile is long, long lost in leagues of rock
What silences begin to weigh upon the world as heavy
    as a mountain,
Towering to the high frown of the sky-blue equator
Whereon the giant sun
Drums on the noon and stuns the wide
Imaginary ocean with his cannonade,

Where shall we find the road to you?
This is the central pole of desolation
Where all the ways lie lost.
Yet here is where you one day came,
Ages ago, a cockle-pilgrim or a fugitive,
Barefoot and poor, or sandalled only
In peacefulness and Gospel-shoon.

How can we make our way to where you are
Facing all day the innocent terror
That shadows us behind this cliff?
What eyes we seem to feel
Reaching toward our backs as frail as tentacles:
Eyes that we turn to face, and never see!
And worse than they:
Who are these mopping legendary creatures,
Smiling and beckoning with hoof and fin:
The centaurs, and their fabled colloquy!
How shall we bear the mewing of these fauns,
Or trust such hairy messengers?

But no, here is no hell-spy.
Here in these white-hot solitudes
We have outstripped the level of deception;
We are beyond the doors of devil-trap.

Therefore we cross the invisible frontier
And come upon your paradise, Father of anchorites,
And your simplicity.

* *

Thus did the great St. Anthony
Make your discovery
Saint, who of all great saints, oh! I most envy!

Alone, alone
In the den by the date tree,
The years told you their numbers one by one
And made more than a century:
But you had forgotten them all.
They were no longer than a quarter hour.

Because God, God
The One I hunt and never capture,
Opened His door, and lo, His loneliness invaded you.

Alone, alone
Sitting in the sunny den-door
Under that date tree,
Wounded from head to foot by His most isolated
    Trinity,
Asking no more questions,
Forgetting how to spell the thought of scrutiny
And wanting no secret
You died to the world of concept
Upon the cross of your humility.

And then your agonizing wounds
Endowed you, in the lair of the forgotten forgers;
Your dark unutterable wounds
Endowed you like a millionaire.

The years went shining by
And there you dwelled,
Grander and wealthier than a fountain,
Quieter and nobler than that old oasis
Of the first, the sinless world.
And the fair springs of your interminable, wordless
    prayer
Went out in secret to transfigure distant cities
With the picture of your charity,
While here the lions came, and bowed their huge
    ferocity,
Gambolled and played to please your gentle gaze
And swept the dust before your den with their
    great manes.

Alone, under the companion and untalking tree
And having lost the key of every mystery
And strayed from the ways of enquiry
You fell upon my God where I and all men
Fear to go walking on such lack of evidence:
But you, slain in the center of your wits,
Passed through the obvious door
Too real for us to find.

And now, old Father of the alone,
Pray us into your stillness,
Into the glory of that faith where you were fed
    by ravens:

Because our minds, lovers of map and line
Charting the way to heaven with a peck of compasses,

Plotting to catch our Christ between some numbered
    parallels,
Trick us with too much logic to the waters
Of the iron Nile
And draw us down to old magnetic Thebes
And to the harlot crowned in martyr-murder,
Throned on the money-colored sea.

SPRING: MONASTERY FARM

When it is spring,
When the huge bulls roam in their pens
And sing like trains;

When the white orchards dream in the noon
And all those trees are dens of light
And boom with honey bees,

The blue-eyed streams
No longer lock their mirth among the icy shales
But run to meet the sun with faces clean.

When Aries
Stands at the crossed ecliptic with a golden cry,
We'll sing the grain that dies and triumphs in
    the secret ground.
Though in our labor and our rational Lent we bend
    our heads
And glaze the dark earth with a shining ploughshare,
Our minds more ardent, hearts insatiable
Than all the amber bees that wrestle in the daffodils,
Sing in the flowers of Your theology.

For, in the sap and music of the region's spring
We hear the picture of Your voice, Creator,
And in our heartspeace answer You
And offer You the world.

For, for all these, their spring is their necessity:

But we have traded April for our ransom and our
     Hundredfold.
Our songs complete those deep, uncomprehending
     choirs.

For, for all these, their spring is their necessity,
Which, by Your Cross and grace, is made our glory
     and our Sacrament:
As every golden instant mints the Christ Who
     keeps us free.

ST. JOHN'S NIGHT

Now where the hills of Languedoc are blue with
    vineyards
Swimming to the brows of the low ridges brown
    as shells,
A thousand villages begin to name your night
    with fires.

The flames that wake as wide as faith,
Opening their fierce and innocent eyes from hill to hill
In the midsummer nightfall,
Burn at the ageless cross-roads these their
Pagan and converted fires.

And the dark shocks of the fair summer's harvest
Rise up in the deep fields
Where for two thousand years, St. John,
Your fires are young among us;
They cry there, loud as was your desert testimony,
Out by the grey olive groves,
Out at the crossing of the vineyard roads
Where once the wheat sheaves wept with blood
In warning to the sickles of the manichees.

And in our hearts, here in another nation
Is made your deep midsummer night.
It is a night of other fires,

Wherein all thoughts, all wreckage of the noisy world

Swim out of ken like leaves, or smoke upon the pools
    of wind.

Oh, listen to that darkness, listen to that deep
    darkness,
Listen to those seas of darkness on whose shores we
    stand and die.
Now can we have you, peace, now can we sleep in
    Your will, sweet God of peace?

Now can we have Your Word and in Him rest?

Prophet and hermit, great John-Baptist,
You who have brought us to the door-sill of your
    wilderness,
You who have won for us
The first faint savor of the world's desertion:
When shall we have to eat the things that we have
    barely tasted?
When shall we have your own vast loneliness's
    holy honeycomb?

You hold in your two hands, lo! more than Baptism:
The fruits and the three virtues and the seven
    presents.
We wait upon your intercession:
Or die we without mercy on the rim of those
    impossible shores?

Kindle, kindle in this wilderness

59

The tracks of those wonderful fires:
Clean us and lead us in the new night, with the power
    of Elias
And find us out the summits of the love and prayer
That Wisdom wants of us, oh Bridegroom's Friend!

And take us to the secret tents,
The sacred, unimaginable tabernacles
Burning upon the hills of our desire!

THE SONG OF THE TRAVELLER

How light the heavy world becomes, when with
    transparent waters
All the shy elms and wakeful appletrees are dressed!
How the sun shouts, and spins his wheel of flame
And shoots the whole land full of diamonds
Enriching every flower's watery vesture with his
    praise,
O green spring mornings when we hear creation
    singing!

The stones between our steps are radium and
    platinum
When, on this sacred day, sweet Christ, we climb
    Your hill;
And all the hours, our steps,
Pray us our way to the high top with silent music
    from the clouds
As each new bench-mark builds us to a quieter
    altitude,
Promising those holy heights where the low world
    will die.

Shall we look back out of this airy treasury
And spill the plenty that we have already in our hands
To view you, cities full of sorcery,
And count the regiments deployed on your grey plain
Where you lie boiling in your smoky wars?

For lo! the music of your treachery
Still plagues us with a sullen rumor in this sinless sun,

And your coarse voice still reaches us.
Sandpapering the silence of our atmosphere.
Shall we turn back to hear those far, far fragile
    trumpets play?

Let us but lean one moment to the witchery of
    your thin clarions
And all our flowery mountain will be tattered with a
    coat of weeds;
And the bright sun, our friend, turning to a
    prodigious enemy,
Will burn our way with curses,
Hardening our hesitation, in that instant, to a
    solid weight,

To bake us white as monuments, like Mistress Lot,
Saltpillars planted on the stony road from Sodom.

EVENING: ZERO WEATHER

Now the lone world is streaky as a wall of marble
With veins of clear and frozen snow.
There is no bird-song there, no hare's track
No badger working in the russet grass:
All the bare fields are silent as eternity.

And the whole herd is home in the long barn.
The brothers come, with hoods about their faces,
Following their plumes of breath
Lugging the gleaming buckets one by one.

This was a day when shovels would have struck
Full flakes of fire out of the land like rock:
And ground cries out like iron beneath our boots

When all the monks come in with eyes as clean
        as the cold sky
And axes under their arms,
Still paying out Ave Marias
With rosaries between their bleeding fingers.

We shake the chips out of our robes outside the door
And go to hide in cowls as deep as clouds,
Bowing our shoulders in the church's shadow,
        lean and whipped,
To wait upon your Vespers, Mother of God!

And we have eyes no more for the dark pillars or
        the freezing windows,

Ears for the rumorous cloister or the chimes of
        time above our heads:
For we are sunken in the summer of our adoration,
And plunge, down, down into the fathoms of our
        secret joy
That swims with indefinable fire.

And we will never see the copper sunset
Linger a moment, like an echo, on the frozen hill
Then suddenly die an hour before the Angelus.

For we have found our Christ, our August
Here in the zero days before Lent——
We are already binding up our sheaves of harvest
Beating the lazy liturgy, going up with exultation
Even on the eve of our Ash Wednesday,
And entering our blazing heaven by the doors of
        the Assumption!

THE TRANSFORMATION: For the Sacred Heart

Heart, in the ardor of Whose holy day
The June is blazing on our world of fruit and wheat,
Smile on our lives, and sanctify them with a new
    love's vintage
And with Your fires vivify our veins.

Lo, the whole humble earth
Bows and is broken with Your loads of bounty,
    and the trees
Fail and give way as we besiege them with a score
    of ladders.
We have no time to turn and hear the tiger-lilies
    all along the field,
Whose outcry warns the world of Love's immense
    invasion
Coming to crowd our continent with full-armed
    shocks.
And look! Those regiments are all around us!
How shall we flee you? You will 'siege us in our
    bursting barns
And force us to a parley in our vines and garden.

Lord, in this splendid season
When all the things that grow extend their arms
    and show the world Your love,

Shall the free wills of men alone

Bide in their January ice
And keep the stubborn winter of their fruitlessness?

Why are we all afraid of love?
Why should we, who are far greater than the grain
Fear to fall in the ground and die?
Have You not planned for minds and wills
Their own more subtle biochemistry?

This is the end of my old ways, dear Christ!
Now I will hear Your voice at last
And leave the frosts (that is: the fears) of my
        December.
And though You kill me, (as You must) more, more
        I'll trust in you.
For though the darkness and the furious waters of
        that planting
Seep down and eat my life away
Yet my dark night both eats and feeds me,
'Til I begin to know what new life, green life springs
        within my bones.

Heart, in the long, daily buryings of anguish
        and of prayer,
Or when I seem to die on the dry burning
        stone, among the thorns,
It is no longer I, but You Who work and grow:
It is your life, not mine that makes these new green
        blades
In the transforming of my soul.
Oh, long before the June, if I but could

I would begin to count my loads of grain,
Hailing the hundreds of the heaven-harvests.
But though they are not yet for man's accounting,
Still in the planted earth I'll hold these hills of gold
Between the blade and the green ear.

RIEVAULX: ST. AILRED

Once when the white clouds praised you, Yorkshire,
Flying before the sun, flying before the eastern wind,
What greenness grew along the waters,
Flowering in the valleys of the purple moor.

Once when the strong sun blessed you, kind as Christ
Slaying the winter mist, delivering the blinded fells,
Banking a million treasures in the waters of the Rye,
Who were the saints who came to claim your
      peacefulness
And build a valley's silence into bowers of permanent
      stone?

The viewless wind came walking on the land like
      a Messiah
Spending the thin scent of the russet heather,
Lauding the flowering gorse and the green broom:
Because this was your spring.
The sky had new-discovered you, and looked and
      loved you
Began to teach you songs to sing upon the day of
      your espousal.
So Rievaulx raised her white cathedral in the
      wilderness
Arising in her strength and newness beautiful as
      Judith.

By night, by night the lamps of York go to and fro
Searching the city with their bleeding eyes
To find where Holofernes lies.

St. Ailred, did you know the dead Assyrian
Whom the new Ladychurch has slain?

Court-craft and pride of heart lie dead
With heads struck off, in Scotland, where were once
    your palace premises.
Go where the tender branches bend and swing
Because the lark and thrush are jeweling the April
    with their hymns,
And spy, between the sunny coppices
The new roof-beams, and smell the curling
    bake-house smoke
And see the barns and ordered yards
And hear the harmony of their various work.

The sun that plays in the amazing church
Melts all the rigor of those cowls as
    grey as stone—
Or in the evening gloom that clouds them through
    those tintless panes,
The choirs fall down in tidal waves
And thunder on the darkened forms in a white
    surf of *Glorias*:
And thence we see the tribes, the tribes go up
To their Jerusalem
Out of the quiet tumult of their fierce Gregorian
    death!

And thence we see the tribes, the tribes go up
And find their Christ, adore Him in His blazing Sion

While the great psalms are flowering along the
    vaulted stones.

Oh, who shall tell the glory and the grace-price
    and the everlasting power
Of what was once the Grey Monks' sacrifice,
When with the slow and ending canticle they broke
    their choirs
And bent them to the ground:

What were your names, you hundred thousand
    cross-cowled nameless saints?
Burning before the Lord upon the altar of your
    poverty and love,
You there destroyed before the face of His great
    Majesty
All the world's armies and her kingdoms and her
    centuries of blood and fire,
And all her palaces and all her treasuries
And the glory of her crowns.

THEORY OF PRAYER

Not in the streets, not in the white streets
Nor in the crowded porticoes
Shall we catch You in our words,
Or lock You in the lenses of our cameras,
You Who escaped the subtle Aristotle,
Blinding us by Your evidence,
Your too clear evidence, Your everywhere.

Not in the groves, not in the flowering green groves
Where the pretty idols dwell
Shall we find the path to Your pavilion
Tented in clouds and fire: ——
We are only following the echo
Of our own lyres.

The wise man's blood
Freezes in every vein and artery
With the blue poison of his own indelible prudence.
And the lover,
Caught in the loop of his own lie
Strangles like a hare:
While the singers are suddenly killed,
Slain by the blades of their own song——
The words that clash like razors in the throat
Severing the tender strings.

For the things that we utter turn and betray us,
Writing the names of our sins on flesh and bone
In lights as hard as diamonds.
And the things we think have sold us to the enemy

Writing the names of our sins on the raw marrow
In lights as sharp as glass.
And our desires,
Uncovering their faces one by one
Are seen to be our murderers!
How did you break your jails, you black assassins?
How did you find us out, you numbered men?

Logic has ruined us,
Theorems have flung their folly at us,
Economy has left us full of swords
And all our blood is gone:
Oh, how like a death, now, is our prayer become!
We lie and wait upon the unknown Saviour
Waking and waking in the guarded tomb . . . .

But the armed ocean of peace,
The full-armed ocean is suddenly within us.
Where, where, peace, did you get in?
And the armed ocean of quiet,
The full armed ocean, stands within us:
Where, from what wells, hid in the middle of our
        essence,
You silences, did you come pouring in?

But all our thoughts lie still, and in this shipwreck
We'll learn the theory of prayer:
"How many hate their own safe death,
Their cell, their submarine!"

"How many hate Your Cross, Your Key, the only one
To beat that last invincible door

That will surprise us, Peace, with Your invasion
And let us in those soundless fathoms where You
  dwell."

CLAIRVAUX PRISON

It is a year of strategy.

The bureaucrats, wiping the blood off their fingers
In the gates of the Temple of Reason,
Have voted to poison the enemy's well.

They know their danger.
They need to throw some dead thing
Into the living waters that were once Clairvaux,
And kill the too clean image
In the heart of such a spring.

Nine or a dozen murderers
And a hundred others with the grime of knavery
    upon them
Go colonize the ancient cloister
On the morrow of the Constitution:
And in the shadows of the broken church,
Each dead soul starts to blossom in his sepulchre
Cursing the comfortable sun.

Heaven, with a strange impassivity,
Shows no particular horror for this grim cartoon:
Lets each new sphinx
Crouch in his iron hermitage
Musing the means to end this leprous noviceship.

And no fire falls.
No brimstone buries these absinthial silences
Or purifies the poisoned sanctuary to a pile of ash.

God is holding you as evidence, Clairvaux;
Saving you, with a most terrifying Providence,
Because you are so true an image of a world
That was untrue to Him.
You are too good a mirror to be broken and destroyed.

Your faithful glass,
Patient of all the grime and blood of the late centuries
Suffers the face of the new liberty,
Frames out the new fraternity for all to contemplate:
Receives equality and holds it fast
With a firm hug of locks,

That those who have never forgotten
The days of Bernard and the first Cistercians
May read the terror of those messages
And fly to keep their freedom in the servitude of
        grace.

NATURAL HISTORY

There is a grey wall, in places overhung
With the abundant surf of honeysuckle:
It is a place of shelter, full of sun.

There, in the middle of September, in the
    vintner's workdays
When the skies begin to change,
Putting away the steams of August 'til the air is loud
    with blue,
The creeping things, in the wise diligence of an
    ascetic season,
Have worked their small momentous wonder,
Prepared their winter's sleep.

O Savior! How we learn Your mercy and Your
    Providence,
Seeing these creatures in their tiny and tremendous
    labor:
Each one diligent and alone
Furling and arming himself in a grey case, the color
    of the wall.

Who told these six or seven creepers how to hasten
    to this place, this safety,
This warm home-haven, better than a Riviera,
And to these stones that will, all winter, never know
    the wind?
Or who has brought them here together,
With no time-table and no calendar,
On this particular day?

Measure the quality of the obedience
With which their natures hear Your thought and
    come,
Each worm hastening as best he can
To die here in this patch of sun.

Leaving all leaves and grasses and the smaller flowers
And all their haunts unseen and summer pastures
They do not stay to study Your command,
    Your mystery,
That this, the only thing they know, must cease
And they must seal themselves in silences and sleep.
See with what zeal they wrestle off their ancient,
    tawny life
And fight with all their might to end their private
    histories
And lock their days in the cocoon.

Walk we and ponder on this miracle
And on the way Your creatures love Your will,
While we, with all our minds and light, how slow
Hard-hearted in our faithlessness, and stubborn as
    the coldest stone!
It was Your St. Theresa struck the deeps
Of this astounding parable——
For all creation teaches us some way of prayer.

Here on the Trappist wall, beside the cemetery,
Two figures, death and contemplation,
Write themselves out before us in the easy sun
Where everything that moves is full of mystical
    theology.

77

Shall we still fear the fight that wrests our way
Free from the vesture of our ancient days,
Killing the prisoner, Adam, in us,
And laying us away to sleep a space, in the
      transforming Christ?

Oh, we, who know from faith and Scripture
All the scope and end of metamorphosis,
Run we like these creatures in their glad alacrity
To our far sweeter figurative death,

When we can learn such ways to God from creeping
      things
And sanctity from a black and russet worm!

A CHRISTMAS CARD

When the white stars talk together like sisters
And when the winter hills
Raise their grand semblance in the freezing night,
Somewhere one window
Bleeds like the brown eye of an open forge.

Hills, stars,
White stars that stand above the eastern stable,
Look down and offer Him
The dim adoring light of your belief,
Whose small Heart bleeds with infinite fire.

Shall not this Child
(When we shall hear the bells of His amazing voice)
Conquer the winter of our hateful century?

And when His Lady Mother leans upon the crib,
Lo, with what rapiers
Those two loves fence and flame their brilliancy!

Here in this straw lie planned the fires
That will melt all our sufferings:
He is our Lamb, our holocaust!

And one by one the shepherds, with their snowy feet,
Stamp and shake out their hats upon the stable dirt,
And one by one kneel down to look upon their Life.

WINTER AFTERNOON

Who shall bridle the winds, in their seven
    directions,
(Now from the north, now from the livid east)
Worrying again these birdless branches,
Storming our forests from the dark south, or the
    west?

We are within the wild doors of another winter
And the black cedars, bowing in the sleet
Sigh all their incoherent music to the tuneless
    country
Waking the deep wood's muffled antiphons.
Walking among the sleepless, iron cemetery crosses,
We praise you, winter, from the deck
Of this our lonely Abbey like an anchored battleship:
While the Kentucky forest
Pouring upon our prows her rumorous seas
Wakes our wordless prayers with the soft din of an
    Atlantic.

And we look up and praise you, winter,
And think of time and the uncertain centuries
Flying before your armies like the coward sky.

And oh! From some far rock some echo of your iron,
    December,

Halts our slow steps, and calls us to the armored
    parapet
Searching the flying skyline for some glare of
    prophecy.

We thought we heard John-Baptist or Elias, there,
    on the dark hill
Or else the angel with the trumpet of the Judgement.

FREEDOM AS EXPERIENCE

When, as the captive of Your own invincible
    consent,
You love the image of Your endless Love,
Three-Personed God, what intellect
Shall take the measure of that liberty?

Compared with Love, Your Triune Law,
All the inexorable stars are anarchists:
Yet they are bound by Love and Love is infinitely
    free.

Minds cannot understand, nor systems imitate
The scope of such simplicity.
All the desires and hungers that defy Your Law
Wither to fears, and perish in imprisonment:
And all the hopes that seem to founder in the
    shadows of a cross
Wake from a momentary sepulchre, and they are
    blinded by their freedom!

Because our natures poise and point towards You
Our loves revolve about You as the planets swing
    upon the sun
And all suns sing together in their gravitational
    worlds.

And so, some days in prayer Your Love,
Prisoning us in darkness from the values of Your
    universe,
Delivers us from measure and from time,

Melts all the barriers that stop our passage to eternity
And solves the hours our chains.

And then, as fires like jewels germinate
Deep in the stone heart of a Kaffir mountain,
So now our gravity, our new-created deep desire
Burns in our life's mine like an undiscovered diamond.

Locked in that strength we stay and stay
And cannot go away
For You have given us our liberty.

Imprisoned in the fortunes of Your adamant
We can no longer move, for we are free.

THE SOWING OF MEANINGS

See the high birds! Is their's the song
That flies among the wood-light
Wounding the listener with such bright arrows?
Or do they play in wheeling silences
Defining in the perfect sky
The bounds of (here below) our solitude,

Where spring has generated lights of green
To glow in clouds upon the sombre branches?

Ponds full of sky and stillnesses
What heavy summer songs still sleep
Under the tawny rushes at your brim?

More than a season will be born here, nature,
In your world of gravid mirrors!
The quiet air awaits one note,
One light, one ray and it will be the angels' spring:
One flash, one glance upon the shiny pond, and then
Asperges me! sweet wilderness, and lo! we are
      redeemed!

For, like a grain of fire
Smouldering in the heart of every living essence
God plants His undivided power——
Buries His thought too vast for worlds
In seed and root and blade and flower,

Until, in the amazing shadowlights
Of windy, cloudy April,

Surcharging the religious silence of the spring
Creation finds the pressure of His everlasting secret
Too terrible to bear.

Then every way we look, lo! rocks and trees
Pastures and hills and streams and birds and
    firmament
And our own souls within us flash, and shower us
    with light,
While the wild countryside, unknown, unvisited
    of men,
Bears sheaves of clean, transforming fire.

And then, oh then the written image, schooled in
    sacrifice,
The deep united threeness printed in our deepest
    being,
Shot by the brilliant syllable of such an intuition,
    turns within,
And plants that light far down into the heart of
    darkness and oblivion
And plunges after to discover flame.

PILGRIMS' SONG

We who have lived too long among your wicked
    children,
The flint-eyed brats who own your splendid streets,
We give you back Stepmother city, to your grey
    and ailing earth!
The millionaires
(Whose limousines sneak to your side as mute as
    gluttons)
The millionaires can have you, Egypt, with your
    onion-breath!

Wait we no longer in the taxi-music of your
    broken gate
Questioning the night our stranger
For maps to measure us a distance from your
    jeweled lights.
Darkness is our delivery. Now die we to your areas
    of grief,
Pointing the arrows of our secret flight
To the wide-open winds of the horizon.

Do your forgotten movies still distil those tears of ice?
Fasten no more these pilgrims to your clock-work
    heart
Nor press them to the beats that tick behind your
    scribbled walls
Where all your sombre ways are a dead-end!

86

You cannot hold us with your imitation arms!

Breathe us no more the measles of your candy kiss
Unlovely relative! We'll lose you by our
      stratagem
In the amazing dusk: by the safe way that you
      ignore: —
We are in love with your antagonist.

And the appalling Cross
The nails that are our liberty become your
      consternation,
'Til we are bled from death to life, and find your
      rival:
And our escaping feet
(That love has fledged with the true wings
Of no imaginary Mercury)
Dance on the air, and run upon the surface of the sea

And climb us out of your dark atmosphere to face
      the blinding east
And conquer all skies with hell-harrowing Christ.

THE LANDFALL

We are beyond the ways of the far ships
Here in this coral port,
Farther than the ways of fliers,
Because our destinies have suddely transported us
Beyond the brim of the enamel world.

O Mariner, what is the name of this uncharted Land?
On these clean shores shall stand what sinless voyager,
What angel breathe the music of this atmosphere?

Look where the thin flamingoes
Burning upon the purple shallows with their rare,
      pale flames,
Stand silent as our thought, although the birds
      in the high rock
Rinse our new senses with no mortal note,
What are these wings whose silks amaze the
      traveller?

The flowering palms charm all the strand
With their supernal scent.
The oleander and the wild hibiscus paint
The land with blood, and unknown blooms
Open to us the Gospel of their five wild wounds.

And the deep ferns sing this epithalame:
"Go up, go up! this desert is the door of heaven!
And it shall prove your frail soul's miracle!
Climb the safe mountain,

88

Disarm your labored flesh, and taste the treasure of
    these silences
In the high coral hermitage,
While the clean winds bemuse you in the clefted
    rock;
Or find you there some leafy Crusoe-castle: dwell
    in trees!

Take down the flagons of the blue and crimson
    fruits
And reap the everlasting wheat that no man's
    hand has sown,
And strike the rock that runs with waters strong
    as wine
To fill you with their fortitude:
Because this island is your Christ, your might, your
    fort, your paradise.

And lo! dumb time's grey, smoky argosies
Will never anchor in this emerald harbor
Or find this world of amber,
Spoil the fair music of the silver sea
Or foul these chiming amethysts:
Nor comes there any serpent near this isle trenched
    in deep ocean
And walled with innocent, flowering vines.

But from beyond the cotton clouds,
Between those lovely, white cathedrals full of sun,
The angels study beauty with their steps

And tread like notes of music down the beamy air
To gain this new world's virgin shore:
While from the ocean's jeweled floor
The long-lost divers, rising one by one,
Smile and throw down their dripping fortunes on
     the sand,

And sing us the strange tale
Of the drowned king (our nature), his return!

THE POET, TO HIS BOOK

Now is the day of our farewell in fear, lean pages:
And shall I leave some blessing on the half of me
    you have devoured?
Were you, in clean obedience, my Cross,
Sent to exchange my life for Christ's in labor?
How shall the seeds upon those furrowed papers
    flower?
Or have I only bled to sow you full of stones and
    thorns,
Feeding my minutes to my own dead will?

Or will your little shadow fatten in my life's last hour
And darken for a space my gate to white eternity?

And will I wear you once again, in Purgatory,
Around my mad ribs like a shirt of flame?
Or bear you on my shoulders for a sorry jubilee
My Sinbad's burden?
Is that the way you'd make me both-ways' loser,
Paying the prayers and joys you stole of me,
You thirsty traitor, in my Trappist mornings!

Go, stubborn talker,
Find you a station on the loud world's corners,
And try there, (if your hands be clean) your length
    of patience:
Use there the rhythms that upset my silences,

And spend your pennyworth of prayer
There in the clamor of the Christless avenues:

And try to ransom some one prisoner
Out of those walls of traffic, out of the wheels of
     that unhappiness!

Poetry and The
Contemplative Life

POETRY AND THE
CONTEMPLATIVE LIFE

The term "contemplative life" is one that is much mistreated. It is more often used than defined, and that is why arguments about the respective merits of "active" and "contemplative" orders generally end nowhere. In the present article I am not talking about the contemplative orders, but about the contemplative life. It is a life that can be led and, in fact, must eventually be led by every good Christian. It is the life for which we were created, and which will eventually be our everlasting joy in heaven. By the grace of Christ we can begin to lead that life even on earth, and many in fact do so begin. Some of them are in cloisters, because the vows and rules of religious orders and congregations make the necessary work of preparation easy and, as it were, almost a matter of course. But many more "contemplatives" are out in the world. A lot of them may be found in places like Harlem and wherever people suffer, and perhaps many of these have never even heard the word "contemplative." And yet on the other hand, not all those who are in contemplative orders are contemplatives. Through their own fault they miss the end of their vocation.

The contemplative life is a life entirely occupied with God—with love and knowledge of God. It can be considered from three points of view, as it were in three degrees. There is first of all possible a kind of natural contemplation of God—that of the artist, the philosopher, and of the most advanced pagan religions.

Then there is the contemplative life in the usual sense of the word: a life in which a baptized Christian, making full use of all the means which the Church puts at his disposal—Sacraments, Liturgy, penance, prayer, meditation, spiritual reading and so on—strives to conform his will with God's will and to see and love God in all things and thus to dispose himself for union with Him. This is *active* contemplation, in which grace indeed is the principle of all the supernatural value and ordination of our acts, but in which much of the initiative belongs to our own powers, prompted and sustained by grace. This form of the contemplative life prepares us for contemplation properly so called: the life of *infused* or *passive* or *mystical* contemplation.

Infused contemplation is nothing but the fulness of the Christian life—the flowering of grace and the gifts and beatitudes which perfect the work of the three theological virtues.

Far from being something esoteric and dangerous, infused contemplation is given us as the normal term of the Christian life even on earth. *Omnis qui ad Dominum convertitur contemplativam vitam desiderat* said Saint Gregory the Great, and he was using contemplation in our sense: to live on the desire of God alone; to have one's mind divested of all earthly things and united, in so far as human weakness permits, with Christ. And he adds that the contemplative life begins on earth in order to continue, more perfectly, in heaven. Saint Thomas echoed him with his famous phrase: *quaedam inchoatio beatitudinis*. Saint Bonaventure goes farther than any of the other Doctors of the Church in his insistence that all Christians should desire infused contemplation. And in his second conference on the Hexaemeron, applying Christ's words in Matthew xii, 42, he says that the Queen of the South who left her own land and traveled far to hear the wisdom of Solomon will rise up in judgment against our generation which refuses the treasures of infused wisdom, preferring the far lesser riches of worldly wisdom and philosophy.

Infused contemplation is an experimental knowledge of God's goodness "tasted" and "possessed" by a vital contact in the depths of the soul. By infused love, we are given an immediate grasp of God's own substance, and rest in the obscure and profound sense of His presence and transcendent actions within our inmost selves, yielding ourselves altogether to the work of His transforming Spirit.

Now whether we speak of contemplation as active or passive, one thing is evident: it brings us into the closest contact with the one subject matter that is truly worthy of a Christian poet: God as He is seen by faith, in revelation, or in the intimate experience of the soul illumined by the gifts of the Holy Ghost.

Consider, for instance, what a tremendous mine of literary inspiration is in the liturgical life. The liturgy itself contains the greatest literature, not only from Scripture, but from the genius of the Patristic and Middle Ages. The liturgy stands at the crossroads of the natural and supernatural lives, and exploits all the possibilities of both in order to bring out every possible meaning and implication that is in them with respect to our salvation and the praise of God. It sur-

rounds those founts of all supernatural vitality, the
Sacraments, with a music that is perfect in its dignity,
and ceremonies that are most meaningful by reason
of their tremendous dramatic simplicity, not to men-
tion all the resources of pictorial and plastic art still
unknown in this land which has never yet possessed
a Chartres or an Assisi.

*

The liturgy is, then, not only a school of literary
taste and a mine of marvelous subjects, but it is infinitely more: it is a great sacramental built around the
six Sacraments which surround the greatest Sacrament
Who is Christ Himself dwelling among us even unto
the consummation of the world.

Christ on the Cross is the fount of all art because
He is the Word, the fount of all grace and wisdom.
He is the center of everything, of the whole economy
of the natural and the supernatural orders. Everything
points to this anointed King of Creation Who is the
splendor of the eternal light and the mirror of the
Godhead without stain. He is the "image of the invisible God, the firstborn of every creature . . . in
Him were all things created, by Him and in Him
. . . He is before all and by Him all things consist
. . . in Whom it hath pleased the Father that all
things should dwell . . . for in Him dwelleth all
the fulness of the Godhead corporeally," that in all
things He may hold the primacy. (Colossians, i and
ii)

And yet Catholic poets and writers generally, although they might possess the key to these treasures
through a love of Christ that would not shrink from

the self-denial required to live a complete and integral Christian life in defiance of the standards of comfort-loving American materialism, prefer to struggle along in the wake of indifferent and mediocre secular models, singing the same old cracked tune that the Georgians inherited from Tennyson and Swinburne and of which even the children of our modern world have long since grown tired.

Of course, it is no wonder that we can't all live like a Saint John of the Cross. But we might at least read him! He is one of the greatest Catholic poets. How many Catholics have ever even heard of him? And yet every time you open a Catholic anthology you will come across something by Alexander Pope who was baptized a Catholic, indeed, and died one, but who wrote as a deist. Contemplation would at least open our eyes to the value of our own tradition, even if we did not have the courage to follow our models to the limit in order to come somewhere near the intensity and perfection of their writing.

No Christian poetry worthy of the name has been written by anyone who was not in some degree a contemplative. But that does not mean that every contemplative is necessarily a great poet. Poetry is an art, a natural skill, a virtue of the practical intellect, and no matter how great a subject we may have in the experience of infused contemplation, we will not be able to put it into words if we do not have the proper command of our medium. That is true. But let us assume that a man already has this natural gift. If the inspiration is helpless without a correspondingly effective technique, technique is barren without inspiration.

Christ is our inspiration, and Christ is at the center of the contemplative life. Therefore, it would seem fairly evident that the one thing that will most contribute to the perfection of Catholic literature in general and poetry in particular will be for our writers and poets to start leading lives of active contemplation. In other words, to lead the full Christian life in so far as they can in their state. That means not necessarily entering a monastery, but aspiring to perfection by the use of all the manifold means that the Church puts at our disposal. It means a solid integration of one's work and religion and family life and recreations in one vital harmonious unity with Christ at its center. The liturgical life is the most obvious example, but it is hard enough to find a parish where the liturgical life is anything more than a bare skeleton. Nevertheless, any man or woman in the world who wants to can make a very fair attempt at becoming an active contemplative and even dispose himself for the graces of infused prayer. And the best disposition is an efficacious desire to arrive at a deep and intimate and personal and loving knowledge of God through Christ.

If such a desire is efficacious, it will not shrink from penance and sacrifices; it will seek them. It will not be bored with prayer, but prayer will become the life of our soul, and we will be able to carry on affective prayer everywhere. We will read Scripture and above all the contemplative saints—John of the Cross, Teresa of Avila, John Ruysbroeck, Bonaventure, Bernard and so on. And God will not make too many difficulties about giving us His wisdom. . . .

It is obvious, then, that contemplation has much to offer poetry. But can poetry offer anything, in return, to contemplation? Can the poetic sense help us towards infused contemplation, and, if so, how far along the way?

*

We have said that the poetic sense may be a *remote* disposition for mystical prayer. This needs explanation. And the first thing that needs to be stressed is the essential dignity of esthetic experience. It is, in itself, a very high gift, though only in the natural order. It is a gift which very many people have never received, and which others, having received it, have allowed to spoil or become atrophied within them through neglect and misuse.

To many people, the enjoyment of art is nothing more than a sensible and emotional thrill. They look at a picture, and if it stimulates one or another of their sense-appetites they are pleased. On a hot day they like to look at a picture of mountains or the sea because it makes them feel cool. They like paintings of dogs that you could almost pat. But naturally they soon tire of art, under those circumstances. They turn aside to pat a real dog, or they go down the street to an air-conditioned movie, to give their senses another series of jolts. Obviously for such people art is not even a remote preparation for even the lowest degree of contemplation.

But a genuine esthetic experience is something which transcends not only the sensible order (in

101

which, however, it has its beginning) but also that of reason itself. It is a supra-rational intuition of the latent perfection of things. Its immediacy outruns the speed of reasoning and leaves all analysis far behind. In the natural order, as Jacques Maritain has often insisted, it is an analogue of the mystical experience which it resembles and imitates from afar. Its mode of apprehension is that of "connaturality"—it reaches out to grasp the inner reality, the vital substance of its object, by a kind of affective identification of itself with it. It rests in the perfection of things by a kind of union which sometimes resembles the rest of the soul in its immediate affective contact with God in the obscurity of mystical prayer. A true artist can contemplate a picture for hours, and it is a real contemplation, too. So close is the resemblance between these two experiences that a poet like Blake could almost confuse the two and make them merge into one another as if they belonged to the same order of things. And yet there is an abyss between them.

Nowhere has this resemblance between the experiences of the artist and of the mystic been better treated than in the long and important article on "Art and Spirituality," by Fr. M. Leonard, S.J., in the "Dictionnaire de Spiritualité." This theologian stresses the dignity of the esthetic intuition practically to the limit. He gives it everything that it is ontologically able to stand. He insists that the highest experience of the artist penetrates not only beyond the sensible surface of things into their inmost reality, but even beyond that to God Himself. More than that, the analogy with mystical experience is deeper and closer still because, as he says, the intuition of the artist sets in motion the very same psychological processes which accompany infused contemplation. This would seem to be too much: but no, it is not. It fits in with the psychology of Saint Augustine and Saint Bonaventure and the latter's notion of contemplation *per speculum*, passing through the mirror of created things to God, even if that mirror may happen to be our own soul.

The Augustinian psychology, which forms the traditional substratum of Christian mystical theology, distinguishes between an *inferior* and *superior* soul. Of course, this is only a manner of speaking. There is only one soul, a simple spiritual substance, undivided and indivisible. And yet the soul in so far as it acts through its faculties, making decisions and practical judgments concerning temporal external things, is called "inferior." The "superior" soul is the same soul, but now considered as the principle or *actus primus* of these other diverse and multiple acts of the faculties which as it were flow from this inner principle. Only the superior soul is strictly the image of God within us. And if we are to contemplate God at all, this internal image must be re-formed by grace, and then we must enter within ourselves by recollection, withdrawing our faculties from external things into this inner sanctuary which is the substance of the soul itself. The majority of people, even those who possess the gift of sanctifying grace, never enter into this inward self, which is an abode of silence and peace and where the diversified activities of the intellect and will are collected, so to speak, into one intense and smooth and spiritualized activity which far exceeds in its fruitfulness the plodding efforts of reason working on external reality with its analyses and syllogisms.

*

It is here that contemplation really begins. It is into this substance or "center" of the soul, when it is suitably purified of images and attachments to sensible things, that the obscure light of infused contemplation will be poured by God, giving us experimental contact with Himself without the medium of sense species, which are, in any case, utterly incapable of apprehending Him.

And yet even in the natural order, without attaining to God in us, the esthetic experience introduces us into this interior sanctuary of the soul and to its inexpressible simplicity and economy and energy and fruitfulness.

Obviously, then, when the natural contemplation of the artist or the metaphysician has already given a man a taste of the peaceful intoxication which is tasted in the supra-rational intuitions of this interior self, the way is already well prepared for infused contemplation. And if God should grant that grace, the person so favored will be much better prepared to recognize it, and to cooperate with God's action within him. And this, as a matter of fact, is a tremendous advantage. The artist, the poet, the metaphysician is, then, in some sense already naturally prepared and disposed to remove some of the principal obstacles to the light of infused contemplation. He will be less tempted than the ordinary man to reach out for sensible satisfactions and imaginable thrills. He will be more ready to keep himself detached from the level of feeling and emotionalism which so easily make the devotion of less wary souls degenerate into sentimentality. The mere fact of the artist's or poet's good taste, which should belong to him by virtue of his art, will help him to avoid some of the evils that tend to corrupt religious experience before it has a chance to take root and grow in the soul.

If only we realized how much the work of the Holy Ghost is impeded in our souls by our insatiable emotional vulgarity—a vulgarity which we innocently bring with us into the House of God and coddle next to our heart our whole life long, never suspecting that it is a dead and poisoned thing. And the saddest of all is that this domestic enemy is nourished and encouraged by so much of the so-called pious "art" that infects the atmosphere of the Church in so many quarters. If there were no other proof of the infinite patience of God with men, a very good one could be found in His toleration of the pictures that are painted of Him and of the noise that proceeds from musical instruments under the pretext of being in His "honor."

Mystical contemplation is absolutely beyond the reach of man's activity. There is nothing he can do to obtain it by himself. It is a pure gift of God. God gives it to whom He wills, when He wills, and in the way and degree in which He wills. By cooperating with the work of ordinary grace we can—and, if we really mean to love God, we must—constantly grow and progress in charity and union with Him by our good works. But no amount of generosity on our part, no amount of effort, no amount of sacrifice will necessarily and immediately gain us progress in mystical prayer. That is a work that must be done by God acting as the "principal agent" (the term is that of Saint John of the Cross). If He is the principal agent, there is another agent: ourselves. But our part is simply to consent and to receive, and all the rest that we can do amounts to the more or less negative task of avoiding the obstacles to God's action, and keeping our own selfishness and sensuality out of His way. Saint Bonaventure tells us in many places that prayer and ardent desire can persuade God to give us this gift, and that *"industria"* on our part can open the way for his action. The term *industria* stands for active purification, and Saint Bonaventure means, by that, precisely the same thing that Saint John of the Cross talks about all through the "Ascent of Mount Carmel," namely the voiding and emptying of the soul, clearing it of all images, all likenesses of and attachments to created things so that it may be clean and pure to receive the obscure light of God's own presence. The soul must be stripped of all its desires for natural satisfactions, no matter how high, how noble or how excellent in themselves. As long as it rests in creatures, it cannot possess God and be possessed by Him, for the love of the soul for creatures is darkness in the sight of God. If we love created things and depend on them and trust in them rather than in God, it will be once again a case of God's light shining in the darkness, "and the darkness did not comprehend it." (John i. 5.)

There is no need to insist on this, since it is the common doctrine of Christian mystical theologians. The one big obstacle to "unitive" of "connatural" or "affective" knowledge of God by infused contemplation (the terms are those of Saint Thomas and his followers) is attachment to human reasoning and analysis and discourse that proceeds by abstraction from sense images, and by syllogizing, to conclusions. In other words, a man cannot at the same time fly in an airplane and walk along the ground. He must do one or the other. And if he insist on walking along the ground—all right, it is no sin. But it will take him much longer and cost him much more effort to get to his destination, and he will have a much more limited view of things along his way. And the even greater obstacle to union with God by pure and infused love, or wisdom, is love of one's own satisfactions, attachment to one's own pleasure, the desire to rest in one's own achievements and in the work of one's own powers and will. If God is to do the work of infusing contemplation into our souls, we must not be busy with our own natural activity, which, *ipso facto*, excludes and prevents this complete freedom of action which God demands in us. All He wants from the mystic is cooperation, peaceful consent, and a blind trust in Him: for all this time, since the soul does not act, it remains blind and in darkness, having no idea where it is going or what is being done, and tasting satisfaction that is, at first, extremely tenuous and ineffable and obscure. The reason is, of course, that the soul is not yet sufficiently spiritualized to be able to grasp and appreciate what is going on within it. It remains with nothing but the vaguest and most general sense that God is really and truly present and working there—a sense which is fraught with a greater certitude than anything it has ever experienced before. And yet if we stop to analyze the experience, or if we make a move to increase its intensity by a natural act, the whole thing will evade our grasp and we may lose it altogether.

*

Now it is precisely here that the esthetic instinct changes its colors and, from being a precious gift becomes a *fatal handicap*. If the intuition of the poet naturally leads him into the inner sanctuary of his soul, it is for a special purpose in the natural order: when the poet enters into himself, it is in order to reflect upon his inspiration and to clothe it with a special and splendid form and then return to *display it to those outside*. And here the radical difference between the artist and the mystic begins to be seen. The artist enters into himself in order to *work*. For him, the "superior" soul is a forge where inspiration kindles a fire of white heat, a crucible for the transformation of natural images into new, created forms. But the mystic enters into himself, not in order to work but to pass through the center of his own soul and lose himself in the mystery and secrecy and infinite, transcendent reality of God living and working within him.

Consequently, if the mystic happens to be, at the same time, an artist, when prayer calls him within himself to the secrecy of God's presence, his art will be tempted to start working and producing and studying the "creative" possibilities of this experience. And therefore immediately the whole thing runs the risk of being frustrated and destroyed. The artist will be cheated of a gift of tremendous and supernatural worth, and be left with nothing—but the experience of an artist. And instead of passing through the sanctuary of his own soul into the abyss of the infinite actuality of God Himself, he will remain there a moment, only to emerge again into the exterior world of multiple created things whose variety once more dissipates his energies until they are lost in perplexity and dissatisfaction.

There is, therefore, a tremendous danger that one who has the natural gift of artistic intuition and creation will be constantly cheated of the infinitely superior gift of the union of the soul with God which surpasses all understanding. He may well receive the first taste of infused prayer, for, as Saint John of the Cross says, that is granted to relatively many souls, and often quite soon in their spiritual life, especially in a monastery: but, because of this tragic promethean tendency to exploit every experience as material for "creation" he may remain there all his life on the threshold, never entering in to the banquet, but always running back into the street to tell the passers by of the wonderful music he has heard coming from inside the palace of the King!

*

What, then, is the conclusion? That poetry can, indeed, help to bring us rapidly through that part of the journey to contemplation that is called active: but when we are entering the realm of true contemplation, where eternal happiness begins, it may turn around and bar our way.

In such an event, there is only one course for the

poet to take, for his own individual sanctification: the *ruthless and complete sacrifice of his art.* This is the simplest and the safest and the most obvious way —and one which will only appal someone who does not realize the infinite distance between the gifts of nature and those of grace, between the natural and the supernatural order, time and eternity, man and God. For the esthetic experience, like everything else temporal, lasts a moment and passes away. Perhaps it enriches the soul with a fuller natural capacity for further experience of the same order—but all such experience will end at death though we will eventually get it back with our bodies. Mystical prayer, on the contrary, enriches man a hundredfold more both in time and in eternity. It purifies the soul and loads it with supernatural merits, enlarging man's powers and capacities to absorb the infinite rivers of light which will one day be his beatitude. More than anything else it forms Christ in the soul. We become the sons of God, says Saint Thomas, (In Matth. v) in so far as we participate in the likeness of God's only-begotten and natural Son, Who is begotten Wisdom, *Sapientia genita.* And therefore by participating in the Gift of Wisdom man arrives at sonship of God. And Saint Bonaventure adds that wisdom, (that is mystical contemplation) is the crowning of Christ's work in souls on earth. *Haec sapientia reddit hominem divinum et Christus venit hanc docere.* This wisdom makes man divine, and it is this that Christ came on earth to teach. (Coll. ii in Hexaemeron.)

The sacrifice of an art would seem small enough price to pay for this "pearl of great price." But there is a further complication, which we can only adumbrate, before closing this article. What if one is morally certain that God wills him to continue writing anyway? That is, what if one's religious superiors make it a matter of formal obedience to pursue one's art, for some special purpose like the good of souls? That will not take away distractions, or make God abrogate the laws of the spiritual life. But we can console ourselves with Saint Thomas Aquinas that it is more meritorious to share the fruits of contemplation with others than it is merely to enjoy them ourselves. And certainly, when it comes to communicating some idea of the delights of contemplation, the poet is, of all men, the one who is least at a loss for a means to express what is essentially inexpressible.

THIS BOOK WAS PRINTED BY
DUDLEY KIMBALL AT HIS PRESS
IN PARSIPPANY, NEW JERSEY